BATHROOMS

MARY GILLIATT

PHOTOGRAPHS BY
BRIAN MORRIS

Alessandro d'Albrizzi, Manfredi Bellati, Anthony Denney
Roger Gain and Paul White

BATHROOMS

THE BODLEY HEAD

LONDON SYDNEY TORONTO

For Sophia
Anne-Louise
and Tom
with love

© Mary Gilliatt 1971
ISBN 0 370 01343 3
Printed and bound in
Great Britain for
The Bodley Head Ltd
9 Bow Street, London WC2
by Jarrold & Sons Ltd, Norwich
Set in Baskerville
First published 1971

CONTENTS

INTRODUCTION

Left: Part of the Roman Bath at Bath.

The history of the bathroom – that essentially personal place – has fluctuated more wildly than that of any other room in the house. In favour, out of favour, used as a meeting place or *salon*, pampered and tended, neglected, banished, kept for relaxation, used only for quick cleansing, a status symbol, a place Victorians would only sidle into, it has emerged, been perfected, submerged and re-emerged again, rising and falling in the thousands of years of our existence like a much abused ballcock.

Providing support for this thesis, an Englishman once complained of his Oxford college that it denied him the everyday conveniences of Minoan Crete. And indeed, Minoan skill in sanitary engineering appears to have far surpassed that of the Chaldeans, the Egyptians and the Greeks, not to mention the Anglo-Saxons who, with one bright exception in the reign of Elizabeth I, had nothing at all to boast about until the nineteenth century.

The Queen's bathroom in King Minos's Palace at Knossos, unearthed by Sir Arthur Evans, was as sumptuous a room as any California wonder, with an enviably shaped and decorated bath – good for all its 3,610 years. Even the water closets in the palace were curiously modern. One of them evidently had a wooden seat and probably an earthenware pan like a modern 'wash-out' closet, as well as a reservoir for flushing water.

Although not quite so talented with their plumbing, the ancient Greeks by all accounts, and in particular Homer's, at least had good hot baths to return to after their travels. And in AD 52, the length of the main aqueducts in Rome totalled some 220 miles, of which only about 30 ran above ground. According to *Clean and Decent*, Lawrence Wright's invaluable history of the bath, fourth-century Rome had eleven public baths, 1352 fountains and cisterns, and 856 private baths. Some private houses at Pompeii are believed to have had as many as 30 taps, and as well as private water-flushed latrines there were plenty of public ones. Rome had 144, Puteoli had one for every 45 persons and Timgad one for every 28.

At its peak, Rome supplied 300 gallons of water per head a day. In London at this moment of time, only 51 gallons per head are used, of which 34 are for domestic

7

and 17 for public use. New York has much the same proportion. But then the scale of the Roman public baths, meeting places as agreeable and as crowded as bars are today, is difficult to grasp. The Baths of Diocletian are said to have held 3,200 people at a time. The vestibule alone was big enough to be converted subsequently by Michelangelo into the splendid church of St Maria degli Angeli. It was opulent, enormous, beautiful. Today, the phrase 'decorated like a public bath' is a term of derision.

Wherever the Romans colonized, which was a considerable part of Europe and Asia Minor, they built their marvellous public baths. And although they built comparatively few private baths in towns, because of the adequate public amenities, they certainly built a number of private baths with complete plumbing systems in the country. Fittings were of bronze, spouts usually taking the form of animals' heads, though dolphins were popular even then.

It is a salutary thought that the Roman occupation of Britain covered a period of well over 300 years, yet almost every civilized custom and habit of living was ignored and effaced within a frighteningly short time. For almost a thousand years after the Roman legions marched away, there was hardly a tap to turn in Europe. The dark ages were dark indeed.

Although it was more normal to go dirty than clean for centuries after this, the monasteries emerged to become a shining example of cleanliness, the virtue that is considered next to godliness. At Canterbury in England, a complete water service was installed in the monastery in 1150. It must have been efficient; that particular monastery was one of the few communities to escape the Black Death in 1349.

A stream for drainage was important for the siting of a monastery, and many of the secret passages which seem clandestinely to have linked monastery with convent are much more likely to have been chaste but practical sewers. Water flushing was rare, but the Abbot at St Albans in England built a stone cistern to store rainwater to serve his 'necessary house' – the medieval latrine. Remains of old monasteries often show rows of pierced stone seats sometimes back to back, with a small division between each, though occasionally they were built in a circle. The bathhouses had plain round or oval wooden tubs made of oak or walnut.

Less holy citizens were not quite so punctilious. Medieval books of etiquette apparently insisted upon the washing of hands, face and teeth every morning, but not upon bathing, though King John of England is said to have taken a bath in a wooden tub about once every three weeks. The shape of the medieval bath was not unlike the average modern structure but was built in this way to allow several people to bathe at once rather than for personal relaxation. Hot water was scarce, so whole families and their guests would bathe together, or at least in quick succession. There are many pictures extant showing communal tubs, some with a tray across the top holding food, and there seem to have been no inhibitions about bathing with the opposite sex nor any feelings of encroachment on privacy.

Right: Hadrian's Villa: Nilus and Colonnade. (Alinari)

Left: Fifteenth-century Italian manuscript painting from *De Sphaera* in the collections of the Bibliotheca Extense, Modena. (Umberto Orlandini)

In the houses of the nobility, the wooden bath often had a decorative fabric canopy over the top and was sometimes padded with linen. Filling and emptying was done with a small wooden bailer. But some royal bathrooms had fixed baths, properly cased in, with, on the very rare occasion, a crude system of running water.

Although the medieval citizen accepted mixed nudity to the point of bathing and sleeping in communal rooms (nightclothes were unknown) it did not stop him being as coy about 'the john', 'the loo', 'the bog', the 'powder room', the 'cloakroom' as we are today, except then it was the 'necessarium', 'the necessary' or 'the garderobe'.

Great houses usually possessed garderobes within the thickness of their walls, each with its own vertical shaft below the stone or wooden seats. The Tower of London has one conveniently near what was the banqueting room. It is about three feet wide, with a narrow window. A stone riser across it contained a wooden seat and a narrow shaft below it turned outwards through a hole in the wall to discharge into the moat below. And just as the myth of the connecting passages between monasteries and nunneries can be explained away by sewers, so many of the so-called priest's hiding holes and private chapels in old houses and castles are much more likely to have been latrines.

For the lower orders there were a few private latrines, more public ones, and public baths had come back into a certain amount of favour via Turkey when the returning crusaders embroidered on the merits of such facilities. All the same, Leonardo da Vinci, in the fifteenth century, did not speak out of turn when he proposed in his plans 'For Ten New Towns' that all drainage of privies and all garbage and street sweepings were to be carried to the river by sewers; and that all stairways in tenement buildings were to be spiral to prevent the insanitary use of stair landings. Furthermore he went on to propose a hot-water system for Isabella d'Aragona, providing for pre-mixed bathwater, three parts hot to one part cold. And for Francis I of France, at Amboise Castle, he suggested a number of water closets with flushing channels inside the walls and ventilating shafts up to the roof.

Alas, like his ideas for submarines, aeroplanes, machine guns and army tanks, these projects came to nothing.

While the sixteenth-century Italians like Pope Clement VII were creating at least the odd sumptuous bathroom with frescoed walls, marble baths and hot and cold water taps, the British sank even deeper into the mire. The only substitute – certainly not an improvement – that they had thought of for the medieval garderobe was the 'close-stool' or 'stool of ease' – more euphemisms! This was a box with perhaps a padded seat, a lid, and sometimes handles to make it more portable. The alternative to this contraption was the floor.

Appalled by this insanitary state of affairs, like Leonardo da Vinci a century earlier, Sir John Harrington, a godson of Queen Elizabeth I and an inventive man, designed a valve water closet complete with seat, pan, cistern, overflow pipe, flushing pipe, valve and a waste with a water seal. But although the Queen had one built at her palace in Richmond (she already had a bathing room at Windsor Castle, wainscotted in glass, to which she was to repair once a month), the invention did not come into public and daily use until it was reinvented some 200 years later. As the dissolution of the monasteries in the reign of Elizabeth's father, Henry VIII, had caused even that tenuous influence on cleanliness to be lost, the sixteenth- and seventeenth-century Anglo-Saxon appears to have led what can best be described as an 'excrementitious' existence. Certainly he was less clean than his medieval counterpart.

In the seventeenth century, even Pepys, that apparently civilized man, kept a 'close-stool' in his drawing room, and in towns all over the British Isles the contents of these close-stools were tipped out of countless upstairs windows on to the streets below to the accompaniment of cries of 'Gardy Loo' – derived, one supposes, from 'Gardez l'eau'. We hardly hear about baths at all.

In France, at this period, bathrooms were built from time to time but they never retained for long the same shape or form. Louis XIII had a wooden bath for most of his life, though he had a grander, colder marble one towards the end. Between 1677 and 1679, Louis XIV installed six baths in his own suite at Versailles and finally added a rose pink marble octagon, 10 feet wide and 3 feet deep, with gilded ceiling, cushions, drapings and a great fabric pavilion. This bath is now in the Versailles orangery after a rather checkered career. At one time during the seventeenth century, Versailles had at least 100 bathrooms, though they were mostly dismantled during the Age of Reason, which was reasonable in almost everything except hygiene.

Madame du Barry's and Marie Antoinette's bathrooms, however, are still extant, and Louis XV's architect, Blondel, explained in his *Maisons de Plaisance*, written in 1738, that the best bathrooms had two baths, one for washing and one for rinsing. Clearly the French at that time were considerably better equipped hygienically than the British. Nor were they modest about the functions of the body. Not only were there apparently 264 *chaises percées* or *chaises nécessaires* at Versailles under Louis XIV, but it was deemed an especial privilege to be received by the monarch sitting on one of these specially adorned and ornamented latrines. And they *were*

Early sixteenth-century French tapestry,
one of a series depicting the life of
the aristocracy. (Musée de Clichy, Paris)

rather elegant. Louis XV had one in black lacquer with a border of mother of pearl, landscapes and birds in gold relief, a red lacquer interior and a padded seat in green velour.

Later, the *chaise percée* in a superior form, in that it could be flushed, was often referred to as *l'Anglaise*, as it was supposed to be of English origin. Unfortunately, Frenchmen interested in the subject seem to have agreed that they had never seen the like in England. Probably the originators of the word had heard rumours of Harrington's Elizabethan invention.

The unselfconscious attitude to the bodily functions in eighteenth-century France showed itself again in the lack of any false modesty about the bidet. Paintings of the period occasionally show ladies using the object, and written records prove that gentlemen were sometimes received by ladies performing their ablutions – a far cry from Americans who, before the last war, forced the Ritz Carlton in New York to take out all the bidets that it had so immodestly and immorally installed.

The French taste did not take effect in England until the second half of the eighteenth century, when washing, at least for the gentry, was gradually transferred from the pump in the backyard to the dressing room. Washstands began to be made as dressing stands, and shaving tables contained mirrors, basins and bidets. Even Hepplewhite designed some fetching little marquetry cases for chamber pots, and less hygienically, but very practically, the sideboard in the dining room often contained a cupboard at one end for pots. Shelves were often concealed behind window shutters to hold chamber pots, for the convenience of gentlemen who stayed on drinking after dinner.

By this time, back in France, the bathroom proper was certainly coming into vogue with the nobility. Napoleon had a splendid bathroom in the Palais de l'Élysée which was really more like a ballroom, and here he took a daily bath – very hot. La Païva, the famous *cocotte*, had a Moorish bathroom in her house on the Champs-Élysées, with a silver-plated bath, turquoise-encrusted taps, walls inlaid with onyx and a cornice of glass stalactites. And then, in 1765, the bathroom really came into its own: an advertisement appeared in a Paris newspaper which actually offered a bathroom as a temptation to buy a house.

In Germany, the Elector's Palace at Baden had a bathroom with a pink and black marble floor, walls of white stucco with panels bordered in amethysts containing reliefs of nymphs. The sunken bath was reached by three steps and water gushed – or so we are told – from the mouths of eight serpents coiled around the edge. The royal apartments in the Pitti Palace at Florence contain a bathroom of such size and magnificence with its statues, inlaid marbles and paintings, that the bath itself seems a sacrilege, a vulgar appendage. But in all these countries, of course, the bourgeoisie had to rest content with water-sellers carrying baths in their cart complete with hot water. There were very few fixed baths. And the poor were still lucky to get a wash at all.

In England it was worse. In 1812, the Lord Mayor of London was not allowed a bath in the Mansion House on the true British grounds that its lack had never been complained of before. Various Council bodies all over the country are still saying

Left: Public bath house-cum-bordello, late fifteenth century.

the same thing in the 1970s, though they will give a grant for a bathless house. In 1832, however, the Mansion House got not only a bath but a hot-water supply with it. Queen Victoria had no bathroom at Buckingham Palace when she came to the throne, though she later added one to each of her royal residences. George IV's great bath in the Royal Pavilion at Brighton was destroyed by her and made into marble mantelpieces for Buckingham Palace. One should mention perhaps that the bath measured 16 feet by 10 feet by 6 feet deep and was supplied with piped sea water. More a swimming-pool than a bath, it may have offended her sense of propriety.

The water closet fared a little more encouragingly, and none too soon. The first patent for one was taken out in 1775 in England by a watchmaker called Alexander Cummings. It was a chancy, precarious affair of intermittent effectiveness, but at least it was a try. Three years later, Joseph Bramah, a cabinet maker, improved on Cummings's invention, and apparently sold 6000 within 20 years. Up until 1890 they were the accepted pattern and a great luxury. Unlike the greater part of Europe, though, in England improved sanitation did not start at the top. The Prince Consort, Queen Victoria's husband, tried to change the commodes inherited from his wife's illustrious forbears in favour of the new water closets and drains, after the bleak discovery of 53 overflowing cesspools under Windsor Castle. But his work was cut short by his death, and not resumed till the next reign. In her grief, Victoria ordered everything to remain where it was so that sanitation and common sense were halted.

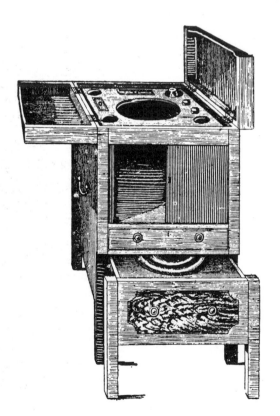

The first complete bathroom in American history is attributed to Latrobe, according to Ishbel Ross in her admirable *Taste in America*. He put a bathtub and a basin together in the same room of a Philadelphia house as early as 1810 and, even more revolutionary, brought the lavatory in from the outhouse to join them and so made America's first three-piece sanitary suite. But Philadelphia had, at that time, by far the best water supply in America.

In 1851, after an extraordinarily long gap, President Millard Fillmore installed the first bathtub in White House history – a move which was considered distinctly reprehensible, 'importing', as it did, 'a monarchical luxury into the official residence of the Chief Executive of the Republic'.

Even when running water became quite ubiquitous and its regular use accepted with equanimity, it was seldom piped above the basement of a house, so that servants had to run up and downstairs with jugs of water, and baths and wash-basins were portable affairs in an astonishing number of shapes: slipper baths (preserving both warmth and decency as its name implies), sponge baths, lounge or full baths, sitting or sitz baths (strictly for the posterior), hip baths, fountain baths (like particularly forceful bidets), and travelling baths.

The revival of the Spa cult in the nineteenth century (its name is taken from the Belgian watering town of Spa), travellers' tales of the Finnish Sauna, and the sun-worshipping of the Swiss, Arnold Rickli, who offered his clients to the sun stretched on tilted boards until they were drenched in sweat, began to popularize the idea of the home steam bath, which was sold in various portable and collapsible models.

Above: Scene in a Women's Bath House.
Woodcut by Torii Kiyonaga. *c.* 1785.

Perhaps, too, the Scandinavian ideal of full exposure of the body to freezing, tingling, cascading mountain streams was the precursor of that American love, the shower. Early shower arrangements began to appear towards the latter half of the century, and were known initially as rain baths.

By the 1880s, Americans were really beginning to show that ascendancy in the hygienic stakes which has earned them their reputation as the most scrubbed and tubbed nation in the world. Although the first actual bathrooms were far from ostentatious with their exposed pipes and scullery-like tiling, things were now beginning to change. During that prosperous period, not only did fixed plumbing begin to appear but the bathroom became a status symbol. Although most bathrooms were still converted bedrooms, new houses were being designed with bathrooms of an equally extravagant size. They were full of stained glass, heavy curtains, panelled woodwork, rugs, *chaises-longues*, armchairs. Some people possessed hooded baths with shower cabinets cased in ebulliently carved mahogany, and all fittings were handsome and solid. The very rich, such as the Morgans, the Astors and the Vanderbilts, were building more and more luxuriously, with gold taps, nickel-plated plumbing and baths carved out of solid blocks of marble. Mrs Potter Palmer, that lady of splendid taste in Chicago, started a fashion for sunken, swan-shaped baths, oval basins and delicate flowery motifs on fixtures, and by 1900 even the patient and less-washed general public were being offered sunken tubs with ornamental tiles, followed by the more utilitarian enamelled bath, making the old mahogany casing lined with lead sheeting, and iron, claw-footed, roll-rimmed tubs quite obsolete.

American hotels were a major influence in popularizing the smaller, functional bathroom. As far back as 1829, the Tremont House Hotel in Boston opened with eight bathing rooms in its cellar, and inside water closets. In 1836, the Astor House opened in New York with 18 bathing rooms complete with piped hot water. In 1853, the Mount Vernon Hotel in Cape May, New Jersey, advertised a bath with hot and cold water for every bedroom. In 1906, the Ritz in Paris, better late than never, did the same. And in 1908, Ellsworth Statler opened his Buffalo Hotel with the slogan, 'A room with a bath for a dollar and a half'. In the same year, in England, that great mansion of the Dukes of Devonshire, Chatsworth, still had only one bathroom.

Two world wars, the proliferation of skyscrapers and tall apartment houses, housing developments, growth in population and increasing pressure on space, not to mention decreasing staff, have all contributed in their way to the reduction in the size of the bathroom, as well as to its functional improvement. It is now considered better to have several small bathrooms just big enough to house the essentials than one luxurious one. Even so, if statistics can be trusted, when the last figures were published a year or so ago more Americans possessed television sets than bathrooms. In England something like one in ten families still do not have a bathroom of their own, and when I lived with a perfectly respectable family of some social pretensions in Paris fourteen years back, no one dreamt of having a bath more than once a week.

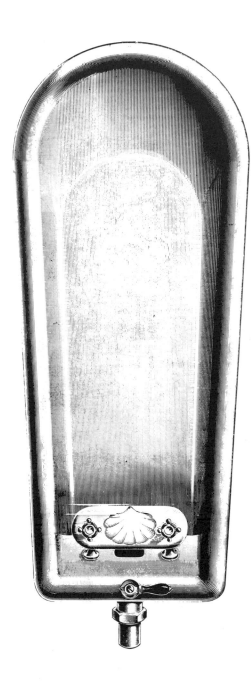

In 1966, Alexander Kira published his report based on a six-year survey for the Centre of Housing and Environmental Studies at Cornell University. In this he suggested that most bathroom equipment was now hopelessly old-fashioned in view of our current technological knowledge. He found lavatory seats too high to be healthy, washbasins too small and too low for efficiency and convenience, baths too cramped and dangerous, showers too awkward and most fixtures unsightly and, on the whole, rather insanitary, and not at all well adapted to the human form.

As a result of this survey, one world-wide manufacturer has already put on the market a complete new range designed to follow Kira's specifications, and others may follow. In 1967, a pre-formed plastic bathroom was introduced at the Montreal World's Fair for Habitat, the apartment development built as part of the Exposition programme, and this bathroom is now imported by many countries to be installed complete. Various other prefabricated bathroom units are being designed and sold, not to mention the increasing number of home Sauna baths, and design groups at several universities from time to time offer *avant-garde* ablutional solutions. One such bathroom of the future, for example, thought up by senior industrial design students at the University of Cincinnati, the University of Illinois, Philadelphia College of Art and Syracuse University, had a basic bath unit which seemed to work rather like a washing machine in that it automatically mixed soap and water for washing at a predetermined temperature (rather like Leonardo's much earlier idea), then followed with a rinse cycle. Other improvements included a floor that cleaned itself and a ceiling that controlled humidity. But in spite of all these technical refinements, or perhaps because of them, bathroom *decoration* (as opposed to design) has reached a new zenith in the last part of the twentieth century.

Never before has there been such a plethora of fixtures, choice of plumbing, and appurtenances. Tiles, wall coverings, towels, floor coverings, carpeting and accessories of every description flood the market. Specialist bathroom shops are opening up everywhere. Bathrooms are being used as studies, sitting rooms, breakfast rooms, dressing rooms, conservatories, solariums, art galleries and anything else that happens to fit in with their primary functions – much as they have always been used, in fact, all down the centuries. They can be ascetic, fantastic, cosmetic, sumptuous, deliberately old-fashioned, almost all wood, thoroughly masculine or just plain feminine.

This book is a record of just such bathrooms – many of them derived from earlier periods – spread over a good part of the world. It does not attempt to be a practical, how-to-do-it book but it does try to show the various decorative possibilities that can be exploited.

One last thought worth lingering on: it is interesting to reflect that when our ancestors did wash they were, until the last century, far less modest, prudish and self-conscious than ourselves. Nor were they ashamed, when they could have it, of luxury and amusement. The bathhouse or room was just as much a place of recreation and leisure as a place to wash in. It was meant to be lingered in; therefore the bathroom is as good a place as any – perhaps a better place than most – to indulge a decorative whim.

EARLY
BATHROOMS

Although there are comparatively few early bathrooms intact enough or accessible enough to be photographed or visited, a study of these few is enlightening. Some of them show clearly where the stimulus for today's more sumptuous baths came from, though they have seldom been equalled. La Païva's bathroom in Paris, and the neo-classical bathroom in the royal apartments of the Pitti Palace in Florence are of a luxury more or less impossible to emulate or even simulate today. Queen Victoria's bathroom at Osborne, on the Isle of Wight, left quite untouched since her death, is interesting for its chaste discomfort – not at all the splendid affair that lesser mortals expect of their monarchs.

Left: The neo-classical bathroom in the royal apartments at the Pitti Palace, Florence, Italy. The bath is a mere (and rather chilly) appendage to the classical statues, inlaid marble and vaulted, ornamented ceiling. To be clean was godly indeed.

Right: La Païva's bathroom in her house on the Champs Élysées, Paris. The famous Second Empire cocotte had this bathroom made for her with silver-plated bath, turquoise encrusted taps, a splendidly tiled floor, walls inlaid with onyx, and a cornice of glass stalactites. It is all extraordinarily rich and lavish.

Left: An early Turkish Bath by Ingres.

Right: A bathroom designed by Anthony Denney for an early eighteenth-century house in Essex, England. Patterned carpet, fabric panelled walls (in a Boussac print), gleaming furniture, glass domes and a roaring fire reflected in the pier mirror provide a comfortably nostalgic room, redolent of Bertie Wooster's pre-war weekends as described by P. G. Wodehouse.

Left: Detail of overmantel and surrounds in Queen Victoria's house at Osborne, Isle of Wight. The mirror is framed a second time by a series of paintings of friends (note the kilted John Brown) and memorabilia.

Right: The bath in Queen Victoria's Osborne bathroom was closed off when necessary by double doors. Walls behind the bath are marble and more rather soulful paintings hang from a brass rail under the cornice.

Right: General view of Queen Victoria's bathroom at Osborne. Looped chintz curtains frame the dressing table. The fireplace used to blaze forth extra heat.

25

Left: Reconstruction of an Edwardian bathroom. From Doreen Yarwood's *The English Home.*

Right: A black marble bath centrally placed below a heavily ornamented mirror reflecting swagged curtains above a marble-topped dressing table and a nostalgic flowered wallpaper, in this Victorian bathroom in the United States.

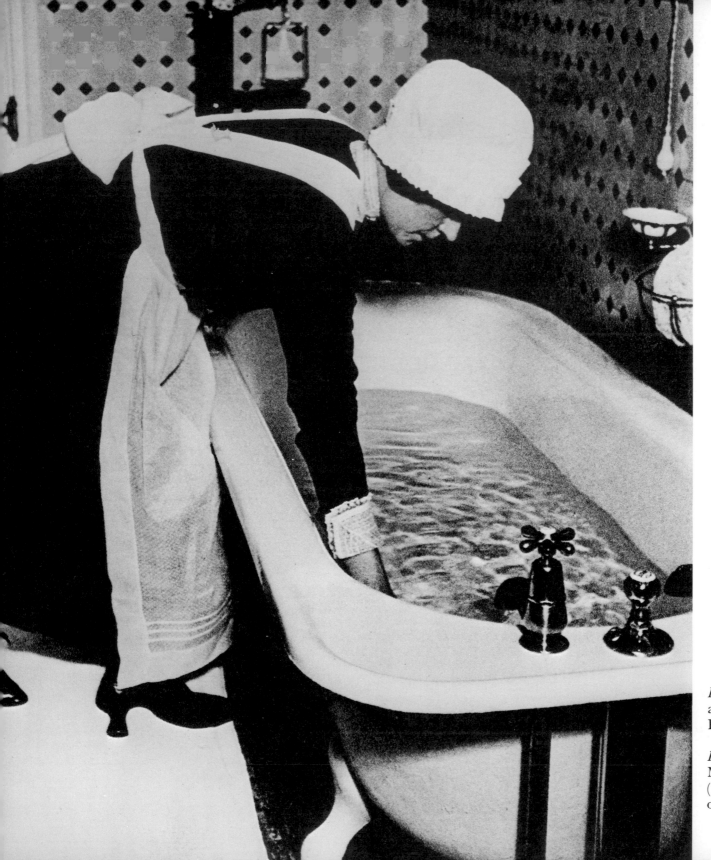

Left: Maidservant filling
an Edwardian bath.
Picture by Bill Brandt.

Right: Mother and Child.
Mary Cassatt.
(Metropolitan Museum
of Art)

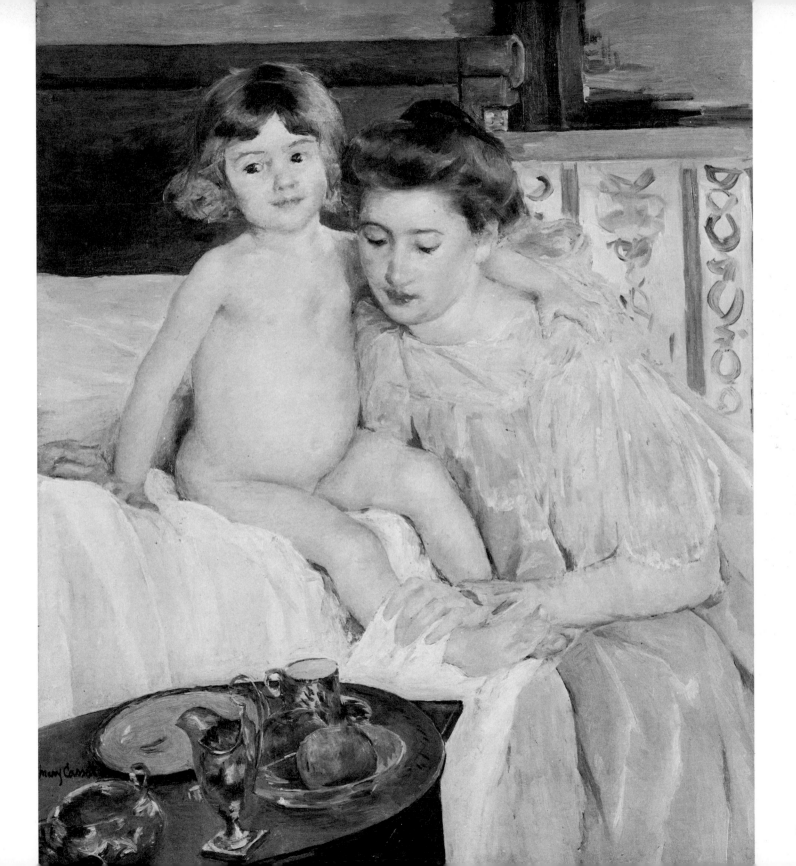

Left: This bathroom survives in Boughton House, Northamptonshire, a seat of the Duke and Duchess of Buccleuch. Panelling, tapestries, Victorian chairs, wood bath surround and a wood enclosed wc of sturdy Victorian type make a handsome room. The light shade was temporarily put up.

Above: A splendid thirties' bathroom in Venice belonging to the Albrizzi family, with *eau de Nil* bath and basin, Breuer furniture, silvered geometric shelving filled with silver objects. Floor and walls are coffee and cream marble, the Breuer chairs are striped in blue and white.

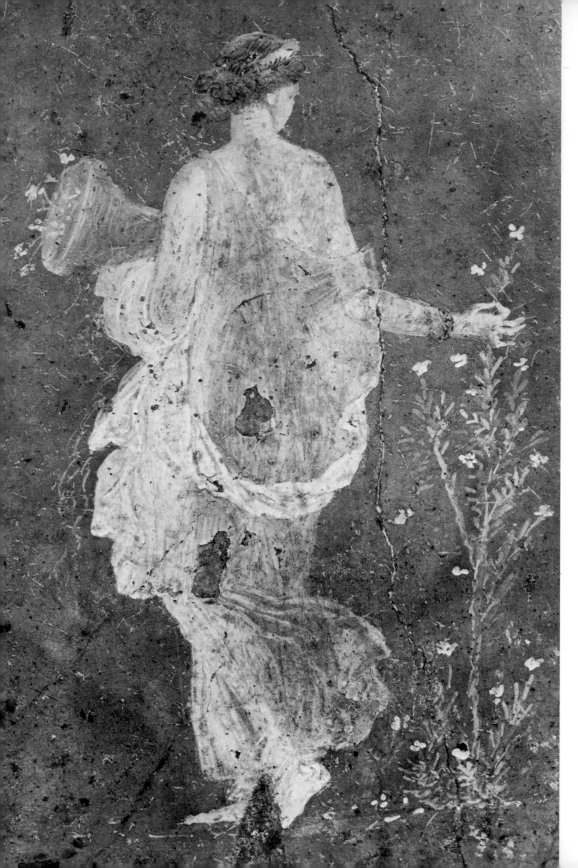

Left: Maiden Gathering Flowers. Wall painting found at Stabiae. (National Museum, Naples)

Right: A rehabilitated bathroom in the Villa dei Vescovi, near Padua, Italy. Vaulted, frescoed walls, marble bath and floor, a font-like wash basin with a pair of candle sconces on either side of the mirror, and what could be an ancient wooden bible rack used as a towel rail.

Left: Opulent thirties' bathroom in creamy marble with beaten glass walls and floor lighting. Pampas grass and fur rug are later additions but have the true period flavour. It belongs to Mr Douglas Villiers in London.

Left: Another Odeon-style bathroom preserved intact by Mr Villiers in his Hampstead house. The reeded glass walls now have their modern equivalent in silvered corrugated cardboard (see the Tynans' bathroom, p. 58). Lighting comes from columns either side of the bath and from a well sunk in the floor. The shower behind its engraved glass dome seems almost hallowed. Chrome is everywhere.

Right: Bergdorf-Goodman's 1920's bathroom in New York City. Black and white marble, solid brass pipes, complicated gilt taps and an elaborate dressing table mirror.

ASCETIC
BATHROOMS

Theoretically, the ascetic bath stems from our prudish inhibitions about luxury and the old adage about cleanliness coming next in virtue to godliness. But ascetic, in my context anyway, need not necessarily mean sparse or bare or unwelcoming. It can be simple, architecturally assured, easily functional, tough, and perfectly, often rather beautifully, fitting for its primary purpose of cleansing.

Left: This African village bathroom in East Hampton, Long Island – perhaps a little smarter than most African villagers' – was designed by Jack Lenor Larsen, the fabric designer. A hole in the slabbed stone floor for a bath, tall pedestalled basins, a wooden roof, African sculptures, dried herbs and sudden exuberant colour in the towels and flowers.

Right: Mexican-style bathroom in California belonging to Edith Head, the costume designer. It is all Indian red octagonal tiles, natural textures and unexpected furniture – at least for the bathroom. It is very spare and beautiful.

Left and right: Simple white marble shower, floor and tub, large areas of mirror glass on the walls and a black lacquered ceiling relieved by a predominantly scarlet painting by Andy Warhol in Fred Mueller's apartment in New York.

Above: Austere fittings, subtle colouring in Mrs Gilbert Hahn's bathroom in Washington. Political posters and bright towels cheer the white walls and tiled floor.

Left: Planes and lines in sculptural intensity. Harold Leeds, head of the Interior Design Department at Pratt Institute, New York, designed his own bathroom in Greenwich village. Thoughtfully arranged bright glass objects in red, lime, opaline and amethyst give gentle contrast.

Right: Concrete bathroom in California designed by architect Arthur Elrod for himself in a harmony of texture and line. Fine herringboned concrete interlaced with blue contrasts with the larger herringbone of the floor.

Left: Simple tiles and bare plaster walls in Spain. Designer Anthony Denney's blue and white bathroom is a cool and immaculate oasis from the strong Alicante sun.

Right: Another view of Anthony Denney's vaulted Spanish bathroom. Walls are whitewashed, floors are brick, windows are deeply recessed, and a row of tiles forms a border.

Right: Italian simplicity. Bare walls, free-standing marble bath, recessed window. The starkness is relieved by the luxuriance of the plant and the graceful lamp.

Above: In Washington, Mrs Mary
Swift has a bathroom-dressing room-
library with black leather sofa and
bath built into one unit, backed by a
wall of terrazzo. A shower unit leads
off a travertine platform built the other
side of the bath.

Right: Concrete shower room in
Lincoln, Massachusetts. Part of the
sculptural, free-flowing concrete house
designed by architect Tom McNulty
for himself and his wife and family.

COLLECTORS' BATHROOMS

The bathroom seems an eminently sensible place to house a collection of almost any sort. Where else can you actually lie and enjoy your possessions? You can examine them from strange angles, contemplate them in private and in peace. And whether you use the bathroom as convenient space for overspill from a large collection of objects or paintings, or whether its often confined space serves as a setting for a more modest gathering, it is equally useful.

Left: Scarlet walls and a black carpet set off a collection of plaster heads slotted into a hive of shelves, and a large black and white abstract in this Milan bathroom designed by Carla Venosta. A tendril-like sculpture embraces the mirror.

Right: A detail of Mr Peter Saunders's huge bathroom-dressing room-study where he has assembled a great number of objects. An aubergine-covered spare bed and aubergine felt walls edged with a brass strip act as a rich and sombre background for the sculpture on the desk, the painting and the horse's head. It is a splendid but unlikely room to be set in the Wiltshire countryside.

Above: Mr Wright Luddington has one of the most distinguished collections of modern paintings and sculpture on the West Coast of America, and his whole house is arranged in a way that has profoundly influenced a number of the world's leading designer-decorators. However, his collection is not only confined to twentieth-century art. This bathroom, with its ochre walls and Chinoiserie, is distinctly eclectic as well as very comfortable.

Right: A comfortable sitting room-bathroom in Mr Norman St John Stevas, M.P.'s eighteenth-century London house. Comfortable chintz sofa, soft carpet, glass cabinets full of important porcelain, and shelves full of part of the owner's noted collection of Victoriana, are joined by a record player, a desk and chest of drawers (not seen), some Cardinal's robes (also not seen), a half bottle of champagne and a thoughtfully placed decanter of port.

Left: A London bathroom designed some years ago by Anthony Denney. Nineteenth-century paintings, posters, prints, plates, stuffed birds, fans, placques, meat-paste lids, mugs, glass, opaline and goodness knows what else are all massed together in a riveting display for the interested bather opposite.

Right: Paintings appear to soar eternally upwards and along in the New York City bathroom designed by Denning and Foucarde. Note the handsome mahogany basin, the intricate glass panelling.

Above : Every room in designer John Dickinson's converted firehouse in San Francisco is brimming over with nineteenth-century *objets trouvés*. The bathroom is no exception.

Top left: Detail of a table in Mr John Dickinson's bathroom, piled high with Art Nouveau bric-à-brac.

Bottom left: Detail of the top of a chest of drawers in Mr St John Stevas's London bathroom. A pair of Queen Victoria's stockings are hung in a frame above.

Above: Detail of the gold basin let into ochre marble in Mr Wright Luddington's California bathroom. The marigolds, the corn and dried grasses, the gold kettle and the various objects make an extraordinary composition.

SUMPTUOUS BATHROOMS

The sumptuous bath presupposes lavish expenditure. Lavish expenditure often, rather unfairly, suggests vulgarity. In any event, these bathrooms are in the grand tradition of comfort, ease, opulence and good planning – rooms meant for enjoyment, relaxation and revival.

Left: Toilet of Venus. François Boucher. (Metropolitan Museum of Art)

Right: Formal French bathroom with rich use of blue and white tiles. Curved marble basins set side by side, a collection of glass, china and paintings, are luxuriously contained by slender pillars and a complicated cornice. In here, bathing could only be elegant and beautifully pristine.

Left: Jon Bannenburg's London bathroom. Mr Bannenburg is one of the most original of today's designers. Here, he has used patterned window-screens to play the light; thick shaggy white carpet, striped towelling on the window seat running the length of the room, and a bath with a travertine ledge wide enough to sit and lounge on, or act as a shelf for plants and various objects.

Above: Lady Irene Astor's bathroom at Hever Castle, England. This was designed by Godfrey Bonsack inside a stone-walled tower room, using one of his fibreglass baths reminiscent of the nineteenth century. Mr Bonsack retained the old oak door and deep stone window embrasure, but lined and tented the stone walls and high ceiling with fuschia pink linen crossed with gold to match the colour of bath, basins and WC (these latter not shown in the picture).

Right: Ken and Kathleen Tynan's London bathroom designed by sculptress Angela Conner who appears to have a particular gift for designing bathrooms. The bath is raised on a platform, and a wicker lounging chair is suspended from the ceiling. A collection of necklaces hang from the pinboard.

Far right: Another view of the Tynans' bathroom. Brown felt walls, silvered corrugated squares of cardboard behind and round the bath covered in perspex, and a perspex canopy above embedded with crustaceae, all go to make a memorable room.

Right: Mr and Mrs Jules Stein's bathroom in Los Angeles is in the best Hollywood tradition: glass shelves against mirror panels are set with a formidable and decorative array of glass bottles and objects which reflect on and on.

Left: Mr and Mrs Thomas H. Guinzburg make superb use of smooth shiny surfaces and reflections in their New York City bathroom. Inviting perspectives mirrored in the glass walls give the room a palatial sense of shine and space, and the coronet of light is reflected from wall to wall, and endlessly on through.

Bottom left: Detail of a well-rounded shower in the Guinzburgs' bathroom which sprays water from the side as well as the top.

COSMETIC BATHROOMS

This is probably the most needed section since it should prove that major changes can be achieved for the minimum expenditure in small dull rooms. Paint and paper, pictures and objects, fabric, thoughtful arrangement and cunning can all be deployed to distract the eye and mind from bad proportions, erratic plumbing, incoherent planning and all the other problems of inherited bathrooms and lack of space.

Left: Bathroom in a late Victorian London terrace house decorated by Paul Anstee. Apricot-papered walls, dark grey carpet, a large-leafed Hosta plant, plenty of pictures and an enormous gilt-framed mirror behind the bath make an otherwise rather poky room seem both spacious and cheerful.

Above: The other end of Paul Anstee's bathroom. A built-up step covered by the carpet like the rest of the floor gives an illusion of space, and a particular sense of ease is provided by the fireplace and Edwardian fender seat.

Opposite: Red and white striped curtains and tie-backs and a matching curtain at the back of the bath in Margaret Cousin's small New York bathroom. A toning stippled paper like peacock's feathers covers the walls and ceiling, and the reeding on the chest picks up the fabric stripes.
Designer: Bill Pahlman.

Left: Painter Ralph Ducasse's bathroom in San Francisco. Warm colours, a collection of absurdities, careful arrangement and long curtains do much to distract the eye from dreary tiles, sprawling plumbing and horrific-looking electric wiring.

Bottom left: A cottage bathroom in England of extreme simplicity. Blue and white Persian tiled paper, white painted door, rush matting on the floor, a few prints on the wall . . . nothing exceptional but notably fresh and pristine.

Above: Fabric on walls, bath panel and rounded basin front in a bathroom designed by David Hicks. A series of well-framed prints, a handsome chandelier and a down-lighter suspended from the ceiling contribute to a very comfortable room.

Right: A long tunnel-like bathroom in an early nineteenth-century apartment in London belonging to Dr Al Kaplan, the film producer. Billy McCarty decorated it very cleverly with chocolate brown felt on the walls and chocolate, green and white paper within the alcove. The floor is peacock blue.

Left: Cosmetic bathroom doubled. Major Tufnell made a double bathroom in his Regency house in Ascot by putting a bath in the room next door and carving an entrance through. A rich olive and orange wallpaper is contrasted with purple perspex bath-panels, and the two rooms are united by a thick white carpet. Pine louvred doors can be slid out to separate the two rooms, and shelves and cupboards have also now got louvred doors.

Right: A pavilion-like feeling achieved with mirror glass and tenting in a country house in England. Pictures are hung on the mirrors between the swags. Designer: David Hicks.

FANTASY BATHROOMS

Bathing is relaxing, and relaxation stimulates the imagination to fantasy. Bathrooms are frequently small so they offer an opportunity for invention at not too great a cost. Rooms in this section are quite disparate. A Moorish splendour in a former Sultan's palace; two cases of pure *trompe l'œil*, one classical, the other wild; and an early copper bath placed in a setting of swans that would have gladdened Leda, and would certainly have pleased that lady of exquisite taste from Chicago, Mrs Potter Palmer, who started using swans in her bathroom at the same time as she was collecting America's first impressionist paintings.

Left: Wild *trompe l'oeil* in an old-fashioned bathroom in London. Irish architect and designer Max Clendinning has brilliantly exploited his space and existing accessories.

Right: A Moorish bathroom in the harem of the former Sultan's Palace in Tangier, designed by David Edge, an English antique and art dealer. Mirrored walls and curved arches reflect a dazzle of colour, light and richness, as well as the chandelier.

Left: Graceful painted copper bath and curving swans in Mrs Mark Brocklehurst's London bathroom. A copper bath was recorded in 1680 and was considered a great improvement on marble. For a long time it was the desired material for such baths as there were until it was superseded by cast iron, which was cheaper.

Right: Classic *trompe l'œil* in France in a small square bathroom. Birds and urns and a perspective of columns and marble cloisters in red, blue and pink marbling with a touch of painted greenery.

Above : Dark blue walls, chestnut carpet, a juxtaposition of circles in mirror, Art Nouveau lampshade, cane chair and straw hat behind the coat stand in architect Vittorio Gregotti's bathroom in Milan. The effect is very light-hearted.

Right : A graceful length of lace drooping from a couronne drapes the marble bath in an old vaulted Italian bathroom. The contrast of insubstantial fabric with solid walls and heavy marble is fanciful, cool and very pleasing.

The wooden tub dates back to medieval England. Then it often had a fabric canopy above it and was padded with linen inside to protect tender posteriors. Today, wood still seems a popular bathroom material though it is not often used for baths themselves. With the exception of one California bathroom shown here with a splendidly smooth wooden tub, it is mostly used for walls, panelling, and general warmth of feeling.

Below : Lattice wood screens, wood panelling around the basin, wood-framed marble floor and wood-framed mirror with a wooden towel rail in journalist Maxine Cheshire's bathroom in Washington. The detailing is very neat and precise.

Right : California redwood walls, panels, window screens, and brown towels and shaggy carpet make up decorator Eleanor Ford's good-looking bathroom in California.

WOODEN BATHROOMS

Left: Cork-panelled walls, wood-latticed ceiling made from trellis-work, a perfect jungle of greenery in the tiny bathroom Paul Anstee decorated for himself in his Buckinghamshire cottage in England. Wooden dolphins coil down the sides of the arched mirror frame.

Right: A silky golden wood tub with central brass taps and a tangle of plants, surrounded by more gold wood walls and ceiling in the San Francisco bathroom belonging to Mr and Mrs Hogle. Living woods tangle outside the window.

Overleaf left: Pine panelling and distinguished paisley wallpaper in photographer Roger Gains's Paris apartment. The arrangement of brilliantly coloured towels in the airing cupboard is a still life in itself.

Overleaf right: Golden pine, red felt walls and carpet, mirrors framed in bird's-eye maple in another French room.

GLASS BATHROOMS

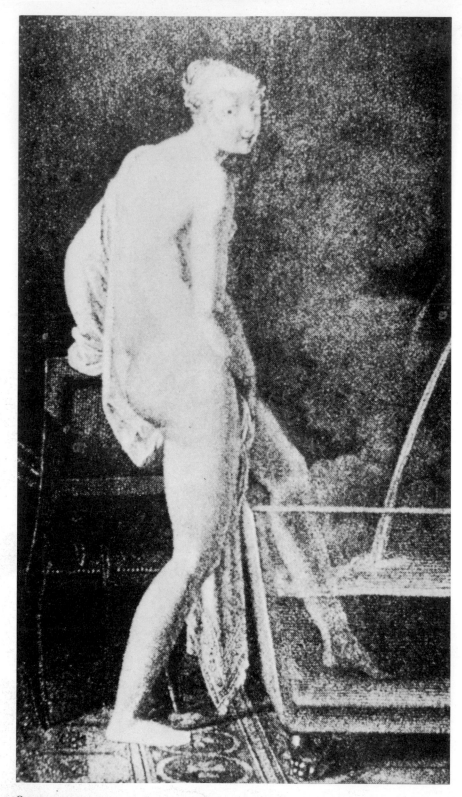

Girard illustrated a marvellous crystal bath in his *Day in the Life of a Courtesan*, and although I have only seen its modern counterpart in clear plexiglass, glass has long played a prominent practical and erotic part in the bathroom. Elizabeth I had her bathroom wainscotted in mirror glass; Napoleon's bath in the Élysée palace is said to have been full of mirrors with painted decoration which must have become steamed up when he had his reputed daily hot bath. The bathroom designed for Eugène de Beauharnais by Boffrand was completely panelled with mirrors. This enlarges a room, reflects, lights and, one hopes, enhances. Equally, mirrors mist up, crack easily, often depress.

Left: A Day in the Life of a Courtesan. Girard.

Right: Old English engraved pub glass is used to panel the London bathroom of Dr and Mrs Sportoletti Baduel. It is delicately used with lace curtains, festoon blinds, an Italian shell basin and WC, and a crimson carpet. Designer: Paul Anstee.

Right : Glass mosaic walls, black and white floor, mirrored cube table and several mirrors make a shining background for a collection of silver and silver lustre in a New York City bathroom designed by Albert Hadley. Everything reflects endlessly.

Left : Glass and beautifully arranged glass shelves separate bedroom and bathroom in this Paris flat designed by Charles Sevigny.

Left : Blue plexiglass rather than glass proper lines all the walls in this bathroom designed by Allessandro d'Albrizzi for the former Miss Vivian Clore's mews house in London.

FEMININE BATHROOMS

We have grown to expect ladies' bathrooms to be soft and pretty, gentle and subtle, fresh and sweet-smelling and beautifully detailed. It is strange how few really feminine bathrooms there are. Is it that ladies, being generous creatures, give in all too easily to the unisex bath? Or is it perhaps that these supposedly feminine qualities have become rare in ladies themselves?

Left: Green chairs, green and white curtains and walls, shaggy white carpet, a discreet telephone, burgeoning plants and a sharp yellow abstract in Mrs Mark Littman's London bathroom. A joint effort with David Hicks.

Above: Gentle blue and white and beautiful detail in this Southampton, Long Island bathroom.
Designer: Leslie Land.

Overleaf: Portugese tiles, pink, aubergine, orange and white fabric for walls, bath curtains, chair seat and tablecloth, white lacquered Chinoiserie Chippendale chairs, tomato coloured carpet and braiding in Mrs Peter Saunders's bathroom in Wiltshire, England, designed by David Hicks. The dressing table is a sheet of plate glass slotted between two obelisks, or rather, one obelisk cut in half to take advantage of the reflection in the mirror set behind. Half urns surmount them and lighting is from up and down-lighters sunk into both ceiling and carpeted floor.

Above: Pale yellow walls, partly mirrored, buff-painted ceiling, pink and white shirred bath skirt and curtains in this subtle London bathroom designed by Elizabeth Meacock for Mrs Anthony Nutting. Prints and paintings are hung on cupboard walls and against the looking glass.

Right: A rich paisley paper in yellows and pinks, a pretty carved wood mirror, and wall lamps for a young girl's bathroom in Mr and Mrs Daniel Schwartz's house in California. It was designed, like the many other bathrooms in this house – all quite different – by Val Arnold.

Far right: Another paisley paper but in blue and white, matched with blue and white towels, in the San Francisco house built by architect Sandy Walker and his wife.

MASCULINE BATHROOMS

The masculine bath, the gentleman's bath. It raises a tangled vision of mahogany and Turkish carpets; clean-cut marble and spare lines; dark colours and warm comfort; the lingering smell of cigar smoke and tangy pine essence and the odd *dégagé* bottle of champagne; idiosyncratic arrangements; a mess of clothes on the floor; a greasy rim around the bath; shaving soap blobbed on the mirror and floors puddled with water. It is all these things.

Left: The emphasis is on quality and texture, relieved by the Greek key-pattern border, in this cool bathroom in the South of France. Basins are set side by side over the wood cupboards.

Right: Dignified marble shower, handsome wood and mirrored walls, wood chair in the New York City house of Howard Perry Rothberg II.

Far left: Mahogany and wallpaper like the inside binding of Victorian books in Mr Mark Brocklehurst's London bathroom. Note the collection of ceramic, naval and military figures, the glass-framed boat, the handsome mirror and general Edwardiana. There is a richly figured Turkey carpet on the floor, not seen.

Left: More mahogany, a strongly figured fabric on the walls in Indian reds and ochres, slim Edwardian lamps, animal paintings and figures and, of course, the Dubuffet, in a bathroom by Anthony Denney in an opulent block of Edwardian apartments in London.

95

Left and above: Architect Ben Thompson's bathroom in Massachusetts has a huge bath that is more like a pool with its handsome wooden frame and mosaic interior. Walls are duckboard, fitted with shower nozzles. The dressing table backs onto the bath wall, and is fitted with wash basin and huge light bulbs around the long mirror.

Clean-cut green marble and mirrored
walls in Mr Daniel Schwartz's
California house. Designer: Val Arnold.

Above: Strong brown and white striped linen walls and bath panel, wicker table, plant holder and basket of lemon soaps in Mr Mark Littman's London bathroom. Designer: David Hicks.

Right: Idiosyncratic New York City bathroom by designers Schule-McCarville. The ceiling is papered with a poster for the last performance at the old Met. Walls are covered in burlap.

This is almost entirely an American invention, and is distinguished from the conservatory bathroom – two of which I have nevertheless included in this section – by the fact that it merges into a courtyard or garden rather than being a specific place to grow plants and bathe. Although in a sense it is an ideal, it is not necessarily as unattainable as ideals often are.

Below and right: Two views of a California bathroom designed by Joseph Esherick for Mr and Mrs Clint Thompson. The glass sliding doors lead out into a jungled yard and the scheme is predominantly yellow and white, cheerful against the window full of tangled green.

INDOOR-OUTDOOR BATHROOMS

Architect Arthur Elrod's bathroom in Palm Springs is a classic example of the indoor-outdoor genre. It is difficult to tell where the disciplined pool-like bath and tiled floor ends and the rocks begin.

The dressing table again in marble, has a stripe through it, which is repeated in the partition wall opposite. Plants inside echo the foliage outside. The mirror is ringed with theatrical bulbs.

The feeling in Arthur Elrod's bathroom
of man-made discipline abruptly
taking over from haphazard nature is
enhanced by the use of concrete,
marble, steel and glass.

Right : Mr Henry Bensinger III's marble bathroom with sunken bath, in Los Angeles, opens out on to a patio protected from the California sun by an awning of yellow and brown striped canvas. A run of wooden cupboards with inset wash basin is surmounted by an antelope head garnered from one of Mr Bensinger's African safari trips. It is unexpected but effective.

Above: Mr William Inge, the play-wright, has a bathroom in Los Angeles with a particular glow caused by the reflection of red walls on white marble floors, continued by rose-painted duck boarding on the floor of the patio immediately outside.

Left: Mr John Wisner's Japanese bathroom at Quoque, Long Island, is beautifully disciplined. It is a subtle harmony of golden wood, off-white ceramic tiles, creamy pebbles, and delicate green, pink and yellow sugar-almond coloured towels.

Left: Mr Peter Panakker's marvellous Los Angeles bathroom-conservatory leads onto a courtyard with an even denser jungle of green. The cream of marble mellows the sunlight to an even gold, exaggerated occasionally by the gilding and the candelabra.

Above: Mr Ivan Moffat, the film writer, commissioned architect Michael Brown to design this very useful adjunct to his London house of conservatory-breakfast room-bathroom high amongst the trees. The bathroom end with its sunken bath is raised from the living area, and can be closed off by louvred doors, which also conceal wc and wash basin (on the left). Blinds shoot up the windows at the turn of a handle, and the outside glass roof is cleaned with sprays of water at the touch of a switch.

Right and left: Two views of a California sitting-room-boudoir bathroom lined almost entirely in marble and designed for Mrs Daniel Schwartz by Val Arnold. The bath is flanked on one side by a luxuriant inner courtyard full of foliage, and on the other by comfortable stools and chairs upholstered in the same beige and white fabric as the long tied-back curtains. It is restful, relaxing, peaceful and cool; the sort of glamorous comfort that one is apt to associate willy-nilly with California, thanks to the early Hollywood image.

A third view of Mrs Daniel Schwartz's
California bathroom or boudoir. The
curved dressing table (which could also
be used as a writing desk) backs onto
the wash-basin unit whose panels are
picked out in the colours of the curtain
and rugs.

Because they are inevitably small, cloakrooms and powder rooms are difficult to photograph, although they are often the most esoteric rooms in a house. Just because of their size, people appear to feel less inhibited about indulging in fantasy, and certainly there can be no excuse for lack of comfort – or at least interest – in so small a space.

Left and right: Prince and Princess Theodore Obolensky conceived the splendid folly of recreating the cloak-room part of Prince Obolensky's family railway coach in their London house. The door *bottom right* is meticulously copied from the original, and almost every other detail is at least correct in feeling.

CLOAKROOMS AND POWDER ROOMS

Left: A delicate silver basin with a rolled and pierced rim set in an old marble washstand in the early eighteenth-century panelled wash-room of Rainham Hall, in Essex, England. Slender candle sconces are set either side of the mirror, and a collection of early objects stand at the side of the washstand top. The room was designed by Anthony Denney.

Right: A dark curved and carved wood counter top with inset basin in the mirrored powder room designed by Val Arnold for the Daniel Schwartzs' California house. A pretty printed wall covering, prints and a handsome mirror make the whole room seem both comfortable and opulent.

Left: A small cloakroom with tiled shower in Windsor. The brown and white tiles are English and an adaptation of seventeenth-century French. The rest of the walls are painted a shiny chestnut brown and there is a chestnut brown carpet to match. There are also odd pictures, plants and a model of Sir Francis Drake's ship.

Right: A collection of glass and opaline on glass shelves in Mr and Mrs John Makepeace's cloakroom near Oxford. Although the photograph had to be in black and white the room is in fact brilliantly coloured with purple paint, an Eastern motif fabric on the wall behind the wash basin, and orange raw silk below the basin counter and behind the WC.